TOP SECRET

PrANK

Hacks

KEEP IT SNEAKY

ACCESS RESTRICTED TO:

....

EWW!

Welcome to the world of
Top Secret Prank Hacks!

This manual is filled with **ideas**, **tips**, and **hacks** for the **easiest** and **funniest** pranking **ever**! As well as prank **DIYs**, you'll find four joke-packed **mini books**, tear-out **prank notes**, and a **top-secret** prank log for **planning**, **recording**, and **rating** your **activities**!

CONTENTS

Prank Rules

Before you get started, read these **important** prank rules:

1 **Pranking** should be kept between **friends**. **Never** prank the **three s's: strangers, seniors**, and **school teachers**!

2 Most pranks require **practice**. Make sure you've **perfected** the **prank** before you spring the **surprise**.

3 If you play practical jokes, you have to be **prepared** to be **pranked back**.

4 **Spread the fun!** If you keep pranking the **same person**, your pranks will cease to be **surprising**.

5 **Check** to make sure your victims have **no allergies** before carrying out pranks involving food, especially nuts.

6 If you make a **prank prop**, make sure you have **permission** to use the materials **first**—even if what you use is yours or it looks like junk!

7 If your prank is **messy**, **CLEAN IT UP** when it's over.

8 **Never**, ever be **mean**. **Pranks** should be **fun** for **everyone**!

The **best pranking** is **harmless** but **super sneaky**! Keep these **hacks** and your pranking plans **top secret** at **all** times, and keep your journal **locked** when it's not in use.

DIY Prop Pranks

Fake Puke

This fake puke recipe is easy and, with different ingredients, can be adapted to make a wide range of sickly splats!

1. Crush up a tablespoon of breakfast cereal in a small cup. Mix it together with cut-up vegetable leftovers.

2. Smooth a piece of plastic wrap over an old magazine.

3. Squirt a blob of PVA glue onto the wrap, and then sprinkle the mix on top.

4. Stir the mixture into the glue with a toothpick.

5. Leave your DIY puke to dry. It will take at least a day, so be patient!

6. When it's thoroughly dry, carefully peel the puke from the plastic wrap. Now you're ready to prank!

Try different **sizes** and **colors** of **splat**. A **small white blob**, *for example*, could easily be mistaken for a **pigeon splat**.

GROSS!

peas

jalapeños

crushed cereal

Freaky Finger

EWW!

There are few things freakier than this classic finger gag!

1. Find an unwanted palm-sized box or small paper cup with a lid. Make a hole in the bottom that's big enough to stick your middle finger through.

2. Put some cotton in the bottom of the cup or box, and then dab it with a little ketchup or red paint and let it dry.

3. Hold the cup or box in the palm of your hand, placing your middle finger through the hole, and pad the box with the dry cotton. Put the lid on the cup or box.

4. Show the cup or box to your friends. When they lift the lid and peer inside, wiggle your finger and watch their faces!

Wonder Worm

This DIY version of a joke-shop prank is a guaranteed gross-out.

1. Unfold a paper clip so you have a straight(ish) piece of wire.

2. Fold the wire around a marker to make a straight-sided horseshoe.

3. Shape the wire around your thumb or finger so it holds firm.

4. Fold the sides down. Then remove it from your finger.

5. Cut a gummy worm in half and push the cut halves into the pointed ends of the paper clip. Put it back on your finger and get pranking.

That's Torn It!

Trick your friend into thinking they've ripped their pants!

1 Take a piece of material nobody wants, such as an old dishcloth or handkerchief. Make a 1 in (2.5 cm) cut halfway down one side (this will make it easy to rip).

2 Hide the rag behind your back or, if it's small enough, in your pocket. When a friend bends over, pull out the rag and swiftly rip it, fooling them into thinking it's their own pants that have split.

SHH...

Increase the likelihood of the person bending by leaving a **"trap,"** such as a **small chocolate bar**, on the **floor**, or **double your pranking pleasure** by combining it with the **next prank**.

Moving Money

Prank your pals as they make for the money!

1 Find an old play-money bill. and scrunch it up so it looks worn. Smooth the bill out, and then attach it with clear tape to a length of black thread.

2 Position yourself behind a couch or armchair, and feed the bill underneath so about three-quarters of it is sticking out the other side.

3 Wait behind the couch until someone enters the room, sees the bill, and bends down to pick it up. When they bend, yank the thread so the bill disappears under the couch. For added effect, have an accomplice ready to add a pant-ripping sound effect *(see above)*.

HACKS

What a Pain!

Fool your folks into thinking you cracked a window!

 Take a piece of plastic wrap, place it on an old newspaper, and smooth it out.

 Using a black marker, draw a zigzag line over the plastic wrap and wait until it is completely dry.

 Place the plastic wrap on a piece of paper and cut around the zigzag (putting the plastic wrap on paper will make it much easier to cut).

 Apply the plastic wrap to a window or one of the surfaces suggested below. Smooth out all the wrinkles. At first sight, it will look as though the glass is cracked!

WARNING!

Never apply the **fake crack** to **anything** that can get **hot**, such as an **oven door**, as it will **melt** and make an **unfunny mess**.

You can use this **prank** with a:
- **TV** screen
- **tablet** screen
- **phone** screen
- **car window**
- car **rear-view mirror**
- bathroom **mirror**

Soap? Nope!

Get your family into a lather!

 Wrap a bar of soap in a layer of plastic wrap. Smooth it out so there are no telltale bumps or lumps.

Leave the soap by the bathroom sink. When the next person goes to wash their hands, they'll be foaming at the mouth with frustration.

KEEP IT SNEAKY

Pencil Pandemonium

They won't be able to get a grip!

1. Smear a little liquid soap lightly over the barrel of a pencil.

 Challenge a friend to a game of hangman.

 Watch their face when they go for the pencil and it falls through their fingers.

Alternatively, bring on the **belly laughs** by giving your **friend** the **bendy pencil** included in this **kit**!

i s t
u m l

p _ a n k e _

Curious Cup

This bug gag will keep them guessing!

1. Tear a hole the size of a small coin from the rim of a paper cup.

 Tear the torn-off piece into small pieces.

 Write *Big spider under cup—please take outdoors* on a sticky note, and attach it to the side of the cup.

 Leave the cup upside down on the bathroom floor or a kitchen counter and scatter the small torn bits around the hole. Your victims will think the spider has chewed its way out of the cup and is on the loose.

Big spider under cup—please take outdoors!

HACKS

Taped-Over Tech

This prank is as easy as it is mystifying!

 Write **Pranked!** on a 1 x 1 in (2.5 x 2.5 cm) piece of paper, and tape it over the sensor underneath a computer mouse.

 Sit back and wait for someone to log on and try to use the mouse. In time, they will turn the mouse over and discover your note.

SHH....

Not a Remote Chance

Here's another low-effort, high-tech prank.

 Write **Pranked!** on a piece of paper small enough to wrap around a battery for a TV remote—probably about 2 x 1 in (5 cm x 2.5 cm).

 When your folks leave the room, quickly take the batteries out of the remote and put them under the seat cushion.

 Roll up your message and put it where the batteries should be.

4 Replace the remote and wait for your folks' reaction when they try to change channels or adjust the volume!

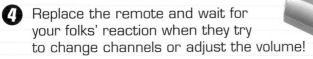

Paper Pranks

Paper has so many quick-and-easy pranking uses. At the back of this manual, you'll find joke notes to tear out or copy. Leave them around the house to fool your family.

I've gone for my math exam.
%̅ = 🖩 + ̄
Adam Upp

Mag Snag

1 Find an OLD magazine. Write **Wow, that's incredible!** on a sticky note, and put it at the top of a random page so it sticks out of the top of the magazine.

2 Stick the marked page to the page before it with small dots of glue. Leave the magazine on a table and wait for someone to try to read the article.

A Hole Lot of Fun

1 Find an OLD magazine and, using a small plate as a template, cut a circle out of a page.

2 Put a sticky note against the page that says **This article is a hole lot of fun!**

Paper Caper

If someone in your home regularly buys a newspaper, save up old copies, and then swap out the front pages so the latest copy has the correct date on the front but old news inside.

DAILY NEWS
READ ALL ABOUT IT

SHH

Out-of-Place Face

Save large pictures of famous faces. Carefully cut one out and stick it to the underside of the toilet seat. The next person to lift the lid will get a celebrity surprise.

KEEP IT SNEAKY

TOP-5 Hole-Punch Pranks

Punch dots have so many uses they deserve their own **Top 5**! Just take a hole punch and some discarded paper (thick paper or thin cardboard works best) and punch away.

Prepare a supply of dots for instant use by filling a small jar or envelope with as many dots as you can.

1 Put a handful in a closed umbrella and wait for your victim to open it up!

HACKS

2 Unroll a roll of toilet paper, scatter dots on the paper, and then carefully roll it back up. You can guess what happens when they pull the paper.

3 Scatter some dots in your friend's upturned hat and wait for them to put it on.

KEEP IT SNEAKY

4 Put dots in between the pages of a book or magazine. When your victim opens the pages, they'll get more than a good read.

5 Scatter some dots inside a shoe. Your victim won't notice a thing until they take them off!

SHH...

Fast Food Pranks

There's a Leek in the Bathtub!

1. Put a leek (the vegetable) in the bathtub.
2. Tell your mom or dad that there's a leek in the bathtub.
3. Follow them in when they go to investigate.

Ice-Cream Scream

1. Use an ice-cream scoop to make two or three balls of mashed potatoes.
2. Freeze or chill the ice-cream balls in the fridge.
3. Serve the potatoes up for dessert with a squeeze of chocolate sauce. They'll look just like ice cream until your victim digs in.

GROSS!

HACKS

Foul Food

1. Find some small plastic tubs and large white sticky labels.

2. Write the names of some gross foods on the labels. You might like to try *Eyeball bites* or *Toenail toasts*.

3. Fill the tubs with real treats.

4. Stick the labels on the tubs and leave them in the fridge or cupboard.

Eyeball bites

Earwax waffles

Toenail toasts

SHH...

Frosty Flakes

1. Pour some cereal and milk into a plastic freezer-proof bowl.

2. Carefully put the bowl in the freezer, and leave it overnight.

3. In the morning, serve up the cereal to your victims for breakfast and watch their faces as they try to dig in.

The Last Straws

Pour about 1 in (2.5 cm) of juice into a plastic cup, and then add a straw. Put the cup in the freezer. When it's frozen solid, take the cup from the freezer and allow the juice to thaw a little so the cup is not too cold to hold. Then fill it up with more juice and ice. Offer the drink to a friend. They won't be able to suck up a sip!

Make holes from the bottom to about halfway up one side of a straw. Put the straw in a glass and fill it with juice so the holes are just covered. Offer the juice to a friend and watch as they struggle to suck it up!

GROSS! Maggot Mayhem

1. Make small holes in an apple with the end of a thick paintbrush.

2. Leave the apple until the holes go brown.

3. Poke small gummy worms (cola flavor is a good choice) into the holes.

4. Return the apple to the fridge or fruit bowl.

Banana Drama

1. Carefully push a toothpick into a seam of a banana, about two thirds of the way up—be careful as toothpicks are sharp. Stop pushing when you feel the end of the stick touch the peel on the other side.

2. Gently wiggle the stick from side to side, being careful not to make the hole in the side of the banana any bigger. Then remove the stick.

3. Offer the banana to a friend. When they peel back the skin, the banana will break in half.

HACKS

Squeezy Teasy

1. Before dinner, collect all the squeeze sauce and mayo bottles.

2. Unscrew the tops, and put a small piece of plastic wrap over each top.

3. Screw the lids back on. When your victims squeeze the bottles, they'll see the sauce but have no clue why it's not flowing.

The **same prank** works perfectly with **shampoo**, **shower gel**, and **liquid soap** bottles.

Cookie Crumble

EWW!

1. Put a tasty cookie on a plate, and slowly drop a teaspoon of water over the top.
2. Leave the cookie for about 15 minutes.
3. Offer the cookie to a friend. It will look perfect but turn to mush as soon as they try to pick it up.

Surely Some Miscake

1. Carefully spoon the frosting off a cupcake to make a hole in the middle.
2. Put a small piece of raw broccoli in the hole.
3. Cover the hole with the spooned-off frosting and serve.

GROSS!

Tricky Toast

1. Using a cookie cutter, make a large hole in the middle of a piece of sliced bread.
2. At breakfast time, ask your victim if they'd like a "hole" slice of toast.
3. When they say yes, serve them the slice with a hole.

Terrible Treats

1. Write the letter E six times on a piece of brown paper or thin brown cardboard.
2. Carefully cut out the E's.
3. Put the letters in a tray with the E's facing the correct direction.
4. Put a cover on the tray, and add a note on the top that says **Please help yourself to brownies!**

KEEP IT SNEAKY

Cereal Switch

1. On Friday evening, take out all the open cereal boxes and swap over the inner bags.
2. Put the boxes out on the counter or breakfast table and let the confusion begin.

Choc Swap

GROSS!

1. The next time your family has a box of foil-wrapped chocolates, wait until no one is looking and take three.

2. Carefully open up the foil, and replace each chocolate with a sprout or green onion.

3. If the vegetables are too big, pull off layers until the size is the same as the chocolates in the box.

4. Put the wrapped onion or sprout in the box with the real chocolates and see who is first to get a savory surprise— just make sure it isn't you!

Milky Way

1. Add a few drops of green food coloring to a carton of milk, hold the top closed, and shake the carton gently.

2. Place the milk on the table and watch your victims get a sour-looking surprise.

HACKS

FUNNY FILLINGS

Nasty 'nut

1. Take two jelly donuts, and carefully make a hole in the bottom of one using a teaspoon handle.

2. Squirt a little mayo or ketchup on the end of a spoon handle, and push it into the donut.

3. Put both donuts on a plate and offer them to a friend, being careful to take your 'nut first.

Cookies 'n' Scream!

1. Take a selection of sandwich-style cookies and gently open them up.

2. Add an edible but unexpected flavor to the cream filling—perhaps a sprinkling of salt and pepper, a slice of pickle, or a little mayo. Then put the cookies back together.

3. Offer them to your friends.

GROSS

No Prop Pranks

Some of the best pranking fun can be had without the need of any special props.

Nothin' Doing

HACKS

This perfect April Fools' prank requires absolutely no props.

1 A few days before April first, tell a friend you've heard of some great April Fools' Day pranks.

2 A little later, say you've thought up the most awesome prank ever but refuse to share it.

3 The next day, say you're deciding who to play the prank on.

4 When April Fools' Day arrives, do nothing except look suspicious. You could try smirking every time you see your pal or suddenly look the other way. You could also keep looking at their bag in a way that suggests you've put something in it. All the while do nothing—the prank is that your pal will spend the day trying to figure out how they've been pranked!

SHH

Yikes! My Thumb Broke!

This classic gag requires a bit of practice, but it's worth it!

1 Hold your right hand sideways away from you with your fingers pointing up. Bend your thumb inward, tucking it against your palm so the top half can't be seen.

2 Bend your left thumb and place it on top of your right thumb so the knuckles join.

3 With your left index finger, cover the section where the two thumbs join.

4 Keep your left index finger in place and slide your left thumb up and down. Your friends will be fooled into believing that your thumb has broken in two!

Pointless Pointing

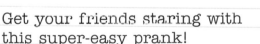

Get your friends staring with this super-easy prank!

1 When you're outside, stop moving, look up, and point at the sky.

2 Wait a few seconds, and then lower your hand and walk on. A few seconds later, look over your shoulder at the people staring at the sky, wondering what you saw.

3 Great places to perform this prank include the park, a playground, the mall, on a busy sidewalk, or the zoo.

Prank Your Roomie

These pranks are perfect for fooling your brother, sister, or roommate.

Move-It Mayhem

1. Sneak into your brother or sister's room and move things around a little. *For example*, switch the books on the shelf so they're in a different order, or move ornaments or trophies onto a different shelf. Be careful not to touch anything that could break.

2. If they notice the changes, look surprised.

3. The next day, move a few more things around.

4. On day three, reveal your prank, and if you're feeling nice, offer to put everything back in the right place.

Scrambled Socks

When your victim is out of the house, go to their sock drawer, separate the socks, and then fold them back together in mismatched pairs.

Alternatively, mismatch **half** the socks, and **hide** the rest in an **unexpected place**, such as **under** your **victim's pillow**. It will be **impossible** to make a pair **without** finding the **hidden stash**.

Clothing Confusion

1. Wait until the coast is clear, and then go to your sibling's drawers. Move the contents of one drawer to another. *For example*, swap the contents of the sock drawer with the contents of the T-shirt drawer.

2. Alternatively, empty a drawer and put its contents in a totally unexpected place, such as under your victim's bedcovers.

3. Leave a drawer empty or fill it with something totally random, such as scrunched up newspapers.

SHH...

Clip-It-Up Chaos!

1. Find about 10 binder clips or clothespins.

2. When the coast is clear, go to your victim's sock drawer.

3. Using the binder clips or clothespins, make a sock string.

4. When your victim pulls out a sock, the clipped-together items will follow.

All Together Now

1. Go to where your victim keeps their shoes and tie all the laces.

2. Alternatively, take the laces out of a pair of shoes and stuff them into the bottom of one shoe. Replace the laces with candy laces or colored yarn.

KEEP IT SNEAKY

candy laces

Inflating Feet

1. Begin the prank by telling your victim that you've read about how, in the summer, the heat makes people's feet bigger.

2. The next day, take two rolled up handkerchiefs or socks and stuff them in the toes of your victim's shoes. Your victim will think their feet have ballooned.

SHH...

Bedtime Surprise

1. Just before bedtime, sneak into your brother or sister's room and place a few surprises under their covers. It could be a (clean) pair of shoes, rolled up socks, or a few crunchy cornflakes (be prepared to clean them up, though).

2. For extra prank value, hide the items under the bottom sheet where they'll be harder to find.

HACKS

Rude Awakening

1. On a Friday or Saturday night, set a wind-up alarm clock for a time when you know your victim will be asleep.

2. Place the clock in a hard-to-see place in their bedroom, such as under the bed or behind a chair.

3. Make sure everyone else in the house is in on the joke or they may not find the wake-up call very funny.

Whoopee on the Go!

There are several different styles of whoopee cushions, but they all give out a satisfying "wooph" when squished. The smallest are great for whoopee on the move—in trains, buses, or planes—as they're easily carried in your pocket and can be activated in your hand. The largest cushions are perfect for placing under a seat cushion for the classic whoopee prank. Some even reinflate themselves, saving valuable pranking time!

Complete the whoopee log, assessing your success using a rating of 1 to 10.

HACKS

Date	Location	Victim	Success
			/10
			/10
			/10
			/10
			/10
			/10
			/10
			/10
			/10
			/10
			/10
			/10
			/10
			/10
			/10
			/10
			/10
			/10
			/10

Bugs, Bugs, Bugs!

Fake bugs, spiders, and other critters have many pranking uses.

HACKS

1 Stick a spider on the underside of a snack-tube lid.

2 Put one or two in your brother or sister's underwear drawer.

3 Tie a string of black thread to a critter's legs and dangle it from a window frame.

4 Hide a scary critter in a shoe.

5 Take a paper cup and tear a small hole around the rim. Put a plastic spider under the upturned cup with some legs sticking through the hole.

6 Hide a bug in the middle pages of a magazine.

7 Put a critter on top of the TV remote.

8 Place plastic maggots next to a serving bowl at dinner.

9 Put a squidgy worm in a bowl under a pile of chips.

10 Leave a fake cockroach next to your mom's dessert.

GROSS

Top Secret Prank Log

Keep a secret record of your pranking plans and achievements here.

Write the name of the prank, who you pranked, when you pranked them, and how successful the pranking was using a rating of 1 to 10.

KEEP IT SNEAKY

Date / Time .... **Location** ....

Prank ....

Who'll be pranked? ....

Equipment needed ....

Notes ....

.... **Success Rating** .... /10

Date / Time .... **Location** ....

Prank ....

Who'll be pranked? ....

Equipment needed ....

Notes ....

.... **Success Rating** .... /10

Date / Time .... **Location** ....

Prank ....

Who'll be pranked? ....

Equipment needed ....

Notes ....

....

....

....

.... **Success Rating** .... /10

Date / Time .... **Location** ....

Prank ....

Who'll be pranked? ....

Equipment needed ....

Notes ....

....

....

....

.... **Success Rating** .... /10

Date / Time .... **Location** ....

Prank ....

Who'll be pranked? ....

Equipment needed ....

Notes ....

....

....

....

.... **Success Rating** .... **/10**

Date / Time .... **Location** ....

Prank ....

Who'll be pranked? ....

Equipment needed ....

Notes ....

....

....

....

.... **Success Rating** .... **/10**

Date / Time .... **Location** ....

Prank ....

Who'll be pranked? ....

Equipment needed ....

Notes ....

....

....

....

.... **Success Rating** .... **/10**

Date / Time .... **Location** ....

Prank ....

Who'll be pranked? ....

Equipment needed ....

Notes ....

....

....

....

.... **Success Rating** .... **/10**

Date / Time .... **Location** ....

Prank ....

Who'll be pranked? ....

Equipment needed ....

Notes ....

....

....

....

.... **Success Rating** .... **/10**

Date / Time .... **Location** ....

Prank ....

Who'll be pranked? ....

Equipment needed ....

Notes ....

....

....

....

.... **Success Rating** .... **/10**

Date / Time .... **Location** ....

Prank ....

Who'll be pranked? ....

Equipment needed ....

Notes ....

....

....

....

.... **Success Rating** .... /10

Date / Time .... **Location** ....

Prank ....

Who'll be pranked? ....

Equipment needed ....

Notes ....

....

....

....

.... **Success Rating** .... /10

Laughter Log

When you hear a good joke or see a good prank, write it down here.

HACKS

SHH...

KEEP IT
SNEAKY

GROSS!

HACKS

Jokes to Go

Make up these joke-packed books for pocket-sized mirth on the move.

KEEP IT SNEAKY

1 Gently press out the pages and book covers. Place the correct covers with the matching spreads.

2 Take one book at a time. Place the cover facedown and stack the pages, facing up, on top of the cover.

3 Fold the pages in half along the spine, and then join them together in the middle with a staple or clear tape.

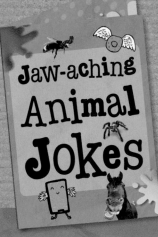

Jaw-aching Animal Jokes

I've gone for my math exam.

Adam Upp

HACKS

The house is a mess!

Dustin D. Furnicha

I've gone for dog food.

Nora Bone

SHH ...

KEEP IT SNEAKY

I've gone to the dentist.

Phil McCavity

HACKS

I've gone to the concert.

Clara Net

I've gone mountain climbing!

Roxanne Stone

EWW!

Meet you
at the zoo.

Aly Gaytor

GROSS

I've gone to my
cooking class.
Sue Flay

I've gone to
buy tissues.

Ronny Nose

SHH

Something looks fishy!

Anne Chovie

The door is jammed!
Paul Hard

SHH...

Have you seen my umbrella?

Wayne Dropps

HACKS

I'm chopping logs!
Tim Burr

KEEP IT SNEAKY

I've gone for a haircut.
Hedda Hair

I've gone to buy salad dressing.
May O'Nays

I've gone to lunch.

Chi Spurger

KEEP IT SNEAKY

Wake me at 6:00!

Earl E. Bird

The power is out!

Alec Tricity

HACKS